World War 2

Submarines

World War 2 Submarine Stories And Accounts: The True Stories Of Battle Under The Dark Seas

Volume 2

World War Two Submarines

Table of Contents

Like FREE books?

Would you like them delivered to you every week?

Do you like non-fiction books on a huge range of different topics?

We send out FREE e-books every week so we can share our books with the world!

We have FREE books every week on AMAZON that we send to our email list.

So if you want in, then visit the link at the end of this book to sign up and sit back and wait for new books to be sent straight to your inbox!

Introduction

I want to thank you for purchasing the book, *"World War II: World War 2 Submarine Stories And Accounts: The True Stories Of Battle Under The Dark Seas"*.

In the many millennia of human civilization, nothing has quite captured man's attention or held it as long as the idea of war does. Long after the sounds of the cannon shots have faded, long after the smell of burning gunpowder has disappeared into the air, war still leaves an indelible mark on the human mind.

The horrors, the pain and the suffering that the soldiers and the victims went through is something we can never truly forget. It is history that is worth remembering and learning from, if only to make sure that something like that never happens again.

We have to turn back the pages of our history textbooks to remember and honor the many sacrifices that the war heroes made. A huge number of people sacrificed their lives; an even bigger number gave up their homes and their dreams to fight enemies on a battlefield that was absolutely unforgiving, cold and cruel.

And of these many battlefields, none were more difficult to face than the ones where the Second World War was fought; millions of people lost their lives to hatred and anger that stemmed from a displaced belief of one's own superiority.

The soldiers who fought in the war were men like you and me who tried to liberate prisoners who had been captured through no fault of their own. Tales of their bravery and their strength can never be trivialized, for they saved thousands of lives while sacrificing their own.

The best part of humanity is that it is ingenious; at times of need, we make do with what we can. The work of the submarines in the Second World War was quite the same – the soldiers who navigated the subs made do with what they could and made war from within the very depths of the oceans and came out successful.

They played a huge role in the Allied Powers bringing down the forces of the Axis Powers and are to be lauded for their amazing strength and courage. They were truly marvels of science, engineered to as near perfect as circumstances would permit, and deployed many strategies to help naval forces defeat the enemy.

In this book, I have outlined much of the role that submarines played in the Second World War. In the initial chapters, I have given you a quick rundown of what submarines actually are, their history and how they operate.

This is followed by a summary of how they worked during the war, before we jump into individual stories of different submarines that fought and made a difference in the war itself.

Thanks again for purchasing this book, I hope you enjoy it!

Chapter 1: Submarine – The Machine

What is a submarine? In the simplest of terms, it is a watercraft that is capable of independent operation under water. The idea of submarines being exclusively a war vehicle is something that developed much after it was initially invented, though when they were invented is something that we are not entirely too sure of.

Legend has it that it was the Greeks who developed rudimentary submarine technology – the story finds its roots in the tale of two men who went into a lake and emerged completely dry, with a candle burning brightly in their hands.

How much of this story is true, one can really only speculate. But the first reliable record we have of a submarine tells of an underwater vessel made by a Dutchman who went by the name of Cornelius Drebbel. The vessel was run manually; men sat inside the machine and rowed with their arms and legs to propel it forward.

Fast-forward to the 18th century, and Nathaniel Symons designed the first true submarine, which had a leather bag that played the role of a rudimentary ballast tank for the sub's ascension and descension.

The first military submarine came into existence when Davis Bushnell built it in 1775 – it was this machine that was capable of independent underwater operation. However, it was not until the American Civil War that submarines began to be used as weapons on the battlefield.

H.L. Hunley was the first submarine that went into battle and claimed a target, even launching a torpedo, though it sank along with its victim.

The problem with most of the initial submarines was the lack of mechanical power required for its propulsion. With the turn of the century and the invention and development in the field of power and energy, submarine technology expanded in leaps and bounds.

The French *Plongeur* was the first vessel to make use of compressed air to move under the water; the Spanish *Ictineo I and II*, made by artist Narcis Monturiol were the first vessels to use a combustion engine with the ability to perform without air.

It was around this time that the Whitehead torpedo came into being, allowing for the submarine to be a properly weaponized vehicle. Add to this development the building of a steam powered engine, later to be replaced by large electric batteries, and one would end up with the porpoise, which were the first weaponized submarines in the world.

However, it was not much of a success, and within a few years, was replaced by the powerful submarines that we see crystallized on the screens today. Large scale usage of the machines began only in the early 1900s.

Slowly, the many Navy's of the world's powerful countries sat up and took notice of the fact that these vessels could do quite a bit of damage on the battlefront. They were sneaky, they were powerful and they had an advantage over the cannons and the ships that Navy's until then had generally consisted of.

Diesel power added to the pros of submarine usage, and the invention of periscopes meant that these vessels were in the perfect position to spy on the enemy, from within the enemy's territory while remaining utterly undetected. Submarines were built excessively in this time, and they were tested and retested to make them perfect.

World War Two Submarines

By the time the First World War rolled around, the submarines were made into quite the formidable force. Let me tell you why they were so effective; let us take a look at the technology that made them such powerful vessels.

The first principle that the submarines operated on was the idea of submersion. A submarine would descend into the water and remain submersed for a length of time – the advantages of this, as a war tactic is obvious. Submersion happens when there is negative buoyancy, which means that the vessel has to weigh more than the amount of water it displaced.

To achieve this, ballast tanks with water and air were used, so that the submarine would remain immersed in the water. There were various technical issues that affected the performance of the submarines, obviously.

The water pressure, as is a well known fact, increases as you travel deeper and deeper into the ocean, putting a lot of stress on the machine, especially since the pressure within the submarine had to be maintained at normal for the people inside.

Intrinsically, that meant a disturbance within its

equilibrium that could be solved only with constant maintenance. The second most important aspect of the submarine was the hull. Designing a perfect hull was no joke.

If it facilitated easy and fast movement, staying underwater would be a problem and if they were designed to remain submerged, then their natural speed would be affected. Over the years, the hull deign has undergone changes to now include single and double hulls. In the latter case, the outer hull withstands pressure differences while the inner hull is made of titanium or strong steel that houses the passengers.

Obviously, designs go only so far without the mechanization to back them up. Propulsion technology was what really kicked the submarines into gear; the earlier submarines were manual, requiring human hands to pull them forward.

Over the years, it developed into something more mechanized, from using compressed air systems to electric batteries, propulsion technology has certainly grown more and more advanced in the recent centuries.

The latest in the field is the usage of nuclear technology,

wherein a small nuclear reactor powers the entire vessel from within.

The machines could get up and run now, but without weapons, they could hardly fight a war. Armament began, as I mentioned previously, with the usage of torpedoes, following which, guns and cannons were added. With the advent of nuclear power, air missiles with cast target ranges are also used in submarine and naval warfare.

Finding your way under the water where one can barely see beyond one's hands is no easy task. Navigation systems then had to be added to the design of submarines if they were to be of any use during wartime.

Early subs were absolutely blind; as time progressed, so did navigation technology. World War II was obviously not a time when GPS was used, but what crude navigation they did have, served them well.

Navigation went hand in hand with communication devices; for subs, this meant the use of the VLF Radio, or the Very Low Frequency Radio. In the time of World War II, this technology – perfected now – was still in the developmental stage, and something called the radio mast was put into play.

The vessels would skim the surface of the seas, and then send up a mast that went above the water levels to convey messages. Since the war ended and the century turned, though, we have come up with better communication systems than we could have previously ever dreamed of.

The final and perhaps the most crucial aspect of the submarines were the life support systems that kept the passengers and the soldiers alive. It began with the air, water and the living spaces provided to them, though it did not end there.

Lifeboats and contingency services had to be provided and over the years, submarine technology has developed enough that the vessels of today produce their own oxygen as well as fresh water to drink on board.

With all these facilities, submarines were designed to be the perfect weapons the navy employed during the Second World War. They were undetected and they were efficient, though in comparison to today's machines, they were ungainly and bulky and more of an eyesore than anything else.

But in terms of the technology of the time, they were

powerful machines that performed extremely well – they played a huge role in the war and contributed much to the Allied Powers' victory. In the following chapter, I will give you a quick run down about the various submarines used by the different nations in the war, before we jump into stories of individual subs.

Chapter 2: Submarines In The War

As I previously mentioned, the popular image is of submarines used as a war vessel or a spy vessel, with the periscope peeking out from beneath the waves to gather information on the enemy. Historically, the use of submarines has been both military and civil, though the latter is so minimal, it is often overlooked entirely, which explains the popular spy machine trope.

In the First and the Second World Wars, submarines played a very important role in mounting successful attacks on ships and defeating opposing navy troops. Deck guns and torpedoes crippled sea trade of enemy nations without mercy; mine laying was a specialty of submarines.

This was due to their covert nature and their ability to approach enemy lines without detection. They laid down underwater mines, which took out more than one ship and won the war for their side. Obviously, they were involved in intelligence gathering, and brought back intimate details of the enemy's plans as well.

With the invention of the ballistic missiles, subs became even more dangerous. They could lie out in the ocean and launch missiles at a target that lay hundreds of miles away from where the sub itself was located. Added to that was the fact that the subs operated in water and sound travels much better in a medium of water than air.

This meant that the submarines could hear ships and other naval machinery coming from miles away. The catch, though, was that a lot of engineers tried their best to reduce their sound footprints.

With all their advantages, it was no wonder that the Allied and Axis Powers took to fighting out the war within the depths of the ocean with submarines. From a purely scientific and technical perspective, the machines of World War II were completely powerless compared to what we have today.

Their speed, endurance, range and the like had nothing on the 21st century's submarines, and yet, they were top of the line, powerful vessels that saw more than their share of battles and destroyed more enemies than we can fathom.

Strangely enough, they spent more time above the water

than below it. It took quite a lot of power to keep a submarine submerged and they would submerge only when it was absolutely necessary to avoid detection.

Let me tell you about the different types of submarines that dominated the bloody battlefield that was the Second World War.

German U-Boats

Germany's U-Boats are probably the most well known submarines of the Second World War. The 'U' in the terms stands for Underwater – an apt description indeed. Earlier on, the German subs spent all their time trying to take out the merchant ships that belonged to Britain.

It was a strategic move, since these merchants' ships supplied the British population with everything from food to weapons. More than 2000 British merchantmen died in these U-Boat attacks.

What is even more interesting is the fact that these battles seemed to be a replay of history from the previous war; even during World War I, Germany had taken to sinking British shipping fleets with their U-Boats.

Karl Doenitz, a veteran of the First War, was the military and naval strategist who led these U-Boats in combat. He trained his men and invented new plans to sink as many ships as possible; his *Wolfpack* plan, where a pack of U-Boats came together to sink a big target instead of getting sunk themselves by confronting it alone, was the cause of many an Allied soldier's death.

U-Boats also had another added advantage; the Enigma Cypher Machine allowed them to send encoded messages that meant that they could talk to each other without getting picked up by their enemies. Without a doubt, this was a huge feather in the Germans' cap.

They captured many an Allied soldier and sunk many an Allied ship with the help of this machine. Unfortunately for the Germans, it was this Machine which also led to the downfall of the U-Boats. They had essentially lumped all their eggs into a single basket.

The only developmental activity the German army undertook was for the betterment of the Enigma Machine. Once the Allies caught on to their plans, they lost their advantage. When Doenitz became head of the German Navy, he upped the production of U-Boats, but by then it was too late.

The British had devised extremely strong anti-sub tactics, along with a genius – Admiral Max Horton, who had been a submarine captain himself and therefore led the British forces in sub warfare with a confidence that was unmatched.

He helped the British defeat many a German U-Boat, but the Nazis were not giving up so easily. It took a long and bloody battle before they finally gave in and the Allied Powers won.

Japanese Submarines

Hands down, Japan was the most technologically advanced power in the Second World War – their underwater vessels clearly reflected their scientific prowess. Their fleet of subs was the most varied and powerful of all the countries involved in World War II.

They had a complete range of submarines including the Type-A and Kairyu class midget subs, the medium range subs to defend the harbors closer to home as well as long range subs that had an immense range, not to mention the supply subs that were built with the express purpose of providing supplies to the soldiers at the front.

Japan also had the I-400 class submarines that carried aircraft as cargo; these subs had the most powerful torpedoes of the time in the world. Added to that was the advantage of the I-201 submarines, which were faster than any other machine at the time.

The irony of this whole situation is that, despite having perhaps the most advanced submarine systems in the world, they could not win the war for the Axis Powers because they did not strategize very well.

The Germans were smarter; they tried to take out merchant ships that were integral to the running of the British economy and thereby take down their enemy. The Japanese, on the other hand, focused on engaging the battleships directly, and lost in that battle, since navy destroyers were far superior to any power submarines might have possessed.

American Submarines

On the side of the Allied Powers, the Americans were the most active in submarine warfare. Navy SEALS took down many an Axis sub, particularly those of the Japanese Navy's. In fact, the American submarines destroyed more than 30% of the Imperial Japanese Navy vessels, including aircraft carriers, cruisers and even one battleship.

The Americans also took a page out of the Germans' book; they hit the Japanese merchant ships hard, making the Japanese war effort costly and expensive. At the end of the war, 48 of the American submarines were lost. But in comparison, they had taken out close to 1500 vessels that belonged to the Axis Powers.

British Subs

The British had the Royal Navy Submarine Service. Unlike the Japanese, who engaged enemy battleships head on, the British submarines were focused on creating blockades to enemy countries; they also took to sinking merchant ships and creating an economic standstill in the Axis Powers.

It was their effort that turned the tide of the war. By the end of the war, it was obvious that the battle had taken place as much in the ocean as it had on land. Submarines had added an unexpected element to navy warfare, and their effectiveness in gathering and dispensing intelligence as well could not be denied.

With this, I have given you the general background of how important submarines were to the War. Now, in the following chapters, let us look at individual submarine stories – of vessels that went to war and fought battles. Some survived, some did not, but all of them contributed to a war effort that left the whole world reeling.

Chapter 3: The USS Nautilus – A Tale of Bravery

On the Allied Powers' side, as I have explained earlier on, it was the American forces that were the most powerful when it came to submarine warfare. Strangely enough, the Allied Forces kept the submarine campaign rather quiet compared to other war efforts, which were made known to the public.

Considering the crucial role subs played in gathering intelligence, this is really not all that surprising. In fact, the U.S. Navy adopted a policy of unrestricted submarine warfare that executed without prior knowledge of the government even.

Black ops were common, and attacking merchant ships and even having domestic merchant ships play roles within the war was a common sight among the Americans' submarine war scenario.

Of the many submarines that fought for the American Navy, the *USS Nautilus* was one of the most powerful. She was the third ship in the United States Navy to bear that name, and she was a Narwhal class submarine – a V-Boat.

She was initially given the name *V-6 (SF-9)*, but then was re-designated and given a hull classification symbol of *SC-2*.

She was officially launched on the 15th of March in the year 1930, and then commissioned on the 1st of July of the same year under the command of Lieutenant Commander Thomas J. Doyle Jr. Before we get into the story of the *USS Nautilus* and how she was part of the war, let me first tell you a little bit about her design so that you can understand what her capabilities were.

The war had progressed to a fierce naval battle with Japan in the western Pacific Ocean, where the subs and naval chargers of the Allied Forces took on the Axis Powers relentlessly. The Japanese, as I have already mentioned, had extremely advanced submarines – they were powerful in a way the Allied Forces had not expected them to be.

It meant that they had to come up with new inventions and ideas to take on the advanced submarines the Japanese Imperial Navy was employing against them. The configurations of the submarines of *V-4, V-5, V-6* were a direct result of this, focusing on the development of long range submarine cruisers that could serve as scouts and lay mines.

The *USS Nautilus* was one such machine; she had a raised gun platform and deck stowage for spare torpedoes. The *V-6* boats had been initially designed with larger diesel engines that were ultimately failures, before they were upgraded with auxiliary engines with charging batteries and a diesel electric system that allowed for increased surface speed.

The *USS Nautilus*, still operating under the name V-6, was based initially out of New London, where she was ordered to conduct submergence tests. She was at this mission until March of 1931, when she was finally given her true name – *Nautilus* – and her hull number of SS-168 on the 1st of July.

She was then sent to Pearl Harbor, where she was turned into a flagship of the Submarine Division 12. A couple of years later, she was reassigned, this time to Subdivision 13 at San Diego in California. There, she served for three years, until in 1938, when she was sent back to Pearl Harbor.

This time, she was involved in training activities; her schedule consisted of regular fleet exercises and training exercises for a decade, until in July of the year 1941, she was sent to the Mare Island Naval Shipyard to be outfitted with the modern technology needed to be part of the war. She was given new radio and communication equipment, her torpedo tubes upgraded and her engines re-installed.

First Patrol

It was now that the battle began for the *USS Nautilus*. She left California on the 21st of April in the year 1942, reaching Pearl Harbor seven days later on the 28th of April. She was under the command of Lieutenant Commander William H Brockman, Jr.

Her mission was to conduct war patrols, and she was to take on the Japanese forces that the Allies knew were coming. On the 4th of June, the vessel was on her usual patrol rounds. She was coming close to the northern boundary of her general lines, near Midway Island, when she sighted masts on the horizon.

It was the Japanese forces that they had been expecting – these planes sighted her the same time she saw them, and they retaliated immediately, strafing the submarine. The *USS Nautilus* had to flee to escape; the natural strength of a submarine came to her aid, and she sank a 100 feet into the sea, disappearing out of the sight of the Japanese forces.

Quietly, she observed them, knowing there was more to come. Just a little while later, she was able to gather efficient intelligence – four enemy ships came into sigh. The Battleship *Kirishima*, the cruiser *Nagara* and two unidentified destroyer ships were forming into a war formation, and it was obvious that they were getting ready for attack.

It was not long before the *USS Nautilus* was sighted again; bombs were thrown at her in an attempt to sink her even as two of the Japanese cruisers closed in for the kill, like a shark circling its prey. *Nautilus* was stealthy and powerful however; she escaped and did not emerge until the attack ceased.

When it was over, she rose to a periscope depth, only to find that she was surrounded by the Japanese ships on either side. But she was not going down without a fight! *Kirishima* was closest and within her range; she fired two of her bow tubes. Unfortunately it did nothing to keep her safe; one missed and the other misfired, leaving her in trouble still.

Her situation was going to get worse; a destroyer headed for her and she had no choice but to sink back into the depths of the ocean to wait out the depth charge attack and try to escape. She stayed under water until the cruiser and the two destroyers were out of range. Finally, the periscope came to the surface of the water again to scope out the danger. This time, they saw an aircraft carrier.

Nautilus then changed her course to close for an attack, but the enemy destroyer followed her, launching six depths charges to attack her. She sank again, trying echo ranging to locate the danger. Outnumbered as she was, there was little she could do but try to escape, and she did just that.

A little while later, when the crew members tried to scope the dangers via the periscope, they found that the seas were devoid of the carrier and the destroyers. Some time passed and around midday, the *USS Nautilus* sighted a damaged aircraft carrier with two escorts by her side. This time, she was not going to go down easy!

Quietly, she moved into an attack position, and an hour later, the battle began. *Nautilus* ended up shooting four torpedoes at the carrier from a distance of around 3000 yards, none of which were truly effective. One did not even run, two ran erratically and did little damage and the fourth one was a complete dud, breaking into two.

But she was meant to be successful in sinking the ship after all – the flames ate at the wood of the ship, even as the crew that was on board jumped overboard to escape the dying ship. Strangely enough, the air flask of the dud torpedo, which was floating about in the water, ended up being a lifeboat to these sailors, who clung to it.

To retaliate, the carrier and her escorts launched a depth charge attack at *Nautilus*, which sank to escape them. A little while later, the periscope was once again put out to scope for danger, and this time, they saw that the carrier, which had begun burning with the torpedoes, was now completely devoid of sailors, who had abandoned her.

A couple of hours later, *Nautilus*, somewhat successful in her mission to ward off the Japanese attack that had been expected, resumed her usual patrol. In the space of a day, she had gotten into two battles, wherein she had launched five of her torpedoes and escaped more than 40 depth charge attacks.

She had seemingly accomplished little, but her commanding officer was nevertheless presented with a Navy Cross for his actions.

Second Patrol

The Nautilus was not quite done with the seas or the war. She resumed her patrol to the west, before which she was replenished and refitted at Midway Island. By the time the 20th of June rolled around, she was working on the coast of the Japanese island Honshu, where she took to sinking destroyers and other Japanese naval forces.

On the 22nd of June, she dealt severe damage to a destroyer that was in charge of protecting the entrance to the Sagami Sea off the coast of Oshima. Three days later, on the 25th of June, she went after another destroyer – *Yamakaze* – and sank it, even dealing powerful hits to another oil tanker that was in the vicinity.

The Nautilus was on a roll; two days after that battle, she engaged a sampan and sank it to the bottom of the ocean. However, her streak of victories was to end soon. On the 28th of June, she took on a merchantman and dealt it a severe blow – but she faced the strongest depth charging attack she had ever seen.

She had to make a hasty retreat to survive, ending up back at Pearl Harbor for repairs, and remaining there until the 7th of August. This first drive in the *Nautilus's* journey during the Second World War drew to a close with that.

Her second patrol began soon after her repairs were over; she took part in the Makin Raid, going back to fight the Axis Powers for the Allies. The *Nautilus* left the waters of Hawaii on the 8th of August. Her time at Pearl Harbor had served her well; she was well outfitted for war again and back in top shape.

This time, she was on a special mission, transporting troops, for a duration of three weeks, and she was not going alone. Sailing with her was another submarine – *USS Argonaut* – and she was under the command of Lieutenant Colonel Evans F Carlson. Along with him, the entire Second Raider Battalion was on board the *Nautilus*.

They would later come to be known as the Marine Raiders or Carlson's Raiders. The *Nautilus* and her passengers landed off Makin Atoll almost a week after they had departed, on the 16th of August.

They were the distraction for the Japanese forces – their mission was to stage a raid so that they would divert Japan's attention towards themselves, away from the Solomon Islands. The morning after they landed, the

Raiders left the *Nautilus* and went to shore, on Butaritari Island in rubber boats.

But the submarine was not out of the action for all that she was left behind! Soon after the Raiders left, she had to provide them covering fire with her guns; the enemy were placed at strategic positions at Ukiangong Point on Butaritari Island and were trying to take out the Raiders.

The Nautilus had to see them to safety, providing them with covering fire until they were in the clear. Soon after, she was engaged in a fight of her own. Enemy ships appeared on the horizon and she had to take them on so that she could survive and await the return of her men.

The few crew members still on board had no choice but to engage these ships; they sank two of them. But still the *Nautilus* was not quite in the clear yet! When the Japanese saw that their ships were not going to sink the powerful submarine, they sent planes to take her on.

Aerial attacks were no joke and 12 planes were launched at the *Nautilus*, which had no choice but to sink into the depths of the ocean to escape a bloody fate. She avoided them, certainly, but two of the 12 planes landed in the lagoon and discharged a number of troops.

The battle was on! The U.S. Marines began to withdraw soon enough, launching their boats to return to the *Nautilus*. A number of them did not make it back; their outboards were damaged, leaving them unable to clear the breakers. Only 7 boats returned to the submarine, with less than 100 men sitting tired and wrung out in them.

The rest of them were stranded on the island, and nine of these soldiers were unfortunately captured by the Japanese and tortured for information before they were executed.

Meanwhile, the *Nautilus* and *Argonaut* set sail back to Pearl Harbor, believing that they had managed to bring back any and all survivors. They were not aware of the men stranded on the island. They returned to Pearl Harbor on the 25th of August, but the *Nautilus* was to set sail again very soon.

Third Patrol

A month after she returned to the Harbor, the *Nautilus* was sent off again, on her third patrol for the Allied

Powers. From the 15th of September to the 5th of
November, she was sent back to Japanese waters.

A submarine blockade chain was being conducted;
stretching from the Kurile Islands to the Nansei Shoto
and the *USS Nautilus* was sent to join the blockade.

This battle was not easy for her; the seas were unforgiving
and they were infested with Japanese carriers and subs.
She had to constantly be on her guard; the periscope
ended up being used almost every minute of the journey,
and her torpedoes were employed without hesitation.

Worse still, the submarine had to be put under
maintenance; mechanical breakdowns became frequent –
not surprising considering the amount of action she was
seeing and the fire she was being put under. Approaching
targets became difficult and she had to endure a lot of
gunfire and attack on this part of her patrol.

Still that did not mean she was useless! She launched
torpedoes at three Japanese merchant ships, which sank
without further ado. She destroyed three sampans, adding
12000 tons to her score. But her journey was only going
to get even more perilous as the days went by.

On the 12th of October, almost a month after she had left Pearl Harbor, she faced a depth charge attack that was pretty heavy and powerful. She escaped relatively unscathed – or so her crew members thought. Two days later, they noticed, to their dismay that she was leaving an oil slick in her wake.

By 19th of October the leak had become too big to not worry about – she was leaving behind a trail for the Japanese to follow. There was little the crew members could do however, except be extremely vigilant and keep an eye out for enemy forces. She moved her patrol to a quieter area where there was little activity on the side of the Axis Powers, and continued her work.

On the 24th of October – two weeks after the leak had sprung up – she sank the *Kenun Maru*, another merchant ship. The battle took quite a bit out of her and she had to head back home. There were no enemy planes in sight and all was quiet – there would be no better opportunity.

She reached Midway Island on the 31st of October, where she was outfitted temporarily to help her on her way back to Pearl Harbor, where she was put through another round of rigorous repairs to get her back into shape for the rest of the war.

Fourth and Fifth Patrols

The *Nautilus* left for her fourth patrol, in the Solomon Islands, on the 13th of December. It lasted for a duration of two months, ending on the 4th of February in 1943. *The USS Nautilus* proved that a submarine could do more than just sink enemy naval carriers; she rescued close to 25 adults and 3 children from Toep Harbor, bringing them back to safety and returning them to their homes.

After that, she went back to her traditional duty of sinking vessels; *Yosinogawa Maru* – a cargo ship – fell to her lethal attacks, along with tankers, destroyers and freighter ships which were damaged by her. In comparison to the previous patrol, this one was relatively easy, and on the 4th of February, when she completed her circuit, she disembarked her passengers and returned to Pearl Harbor for repairs.

This time, though, her time to recuperate was short – she stayed at the Harbor only for five days before she was sent off again, this time heading north to Alaska, where she was stationed at the Dutch Harbor.

In April, at the Dutch Harbor, she began her new job of instructing the 7th Infantry Division Provisional Scout

Battalion in amphibious landings. 109 of the Scouts she trained went on board and together, they left for Attu, where she completed her fifth patrol.

Sixth Patrol

Returning to Mare Island and undergoing repairs took up almost the entire summer, following which the *Nautilus* was sent on her 6th war patrol to the Gilbert Islands. Her mission was to conduct photo-reconnaissance; these islands had been reinforced, especially Tarawa, since the submarines had had their excursion there in 1942.

The invasion of Tarawa required intelligence and the *Nautilus* gathered critical information that would prove vital to the upcoming battle. She sent continuous panoramic pictures of the coastlines, corrected nautical charts, and brought back valuable intelligence that would greatly improve the Allied Powers' chances of taking Tarawa.

As she was circling Tarawa for some last minute recon – to get information on the weather and wave conditions, landing hazards and the outcome of the latest bombs – she was put into grave peril. Ironically, the danger came not from the Axis Powers, but her own Navy.

The *USS Ringgold* sighted her from a distance, and assuming that she was an enemy sub, the destroyer fired at her, sending a 5-inch shell through the conning tower. The main induction valve of the *Nautilus* was damaged, but she was not giving up on her mission! She dived beneath the waters, where her damage control crew got to work. They patched her up as best they could, allowing her to continue her work.

Seventh Patrol

She did not return to Pearl Harbor, continuing on to her seventh patrol. She landed a 78-man scouting party on Abemama, where they went to work gathering intelligence they would require for the upcoming siege.

A couple of days later, on the night of 21st November, the *Nautilus* deposited all of her passengers safely on an island off the coast of Abemama Atoll. That very day, she would also provide fire to the men trying to take out a garrison of enemy fighters from within their bunkers.

Out of the 25 men, the Marines were able to coax out 14, whom they killed. The rest committed suicide. Thanks to the *Nautilus*, though, the island of Abemama had been captured even before the main assault team arrived on the scene. The soldiers who had taken it had already begun the preparations to convert it into an air base.

Her job at the Abemama Island finished, she returned to Pearl Harbor for more repairs and to prepare for her eighth patrol of the Second World War.

Eight Patrol

This was to be conducted at the north of Palau, west of the Mariana Islands. The *Nautilus* left in January and the patrol lasted for three months, ending only on the 21st of March 1944. Again, she proved a fierce fighter, taking out one cargo ship, another merchant ship and then damaging three other ships severely.

Once her job there was done, the *Nautilus* left for Brisbane, Australia, where she was to start a series of special missions that would support the guerrilla and recon missions being conducted in the Philippines.

Ninth-Fourteenth Patrols

USS Nautilus's ninth patrol lasted from the 29th of May to the 11th of June, where she carried supplies to Colonel R.V. Bowler on Mindanao Island in the Philippines. After that, until the 27th of June, she transported more cargo to the Negros Island and once again took to rescuing people.

She evacuated a number of refugees and took them to Darwin, Australia ending her tenth patrol there. The eleventh was also a supply run, doubling as a recon mission – she carried stores and supplies to Colonel Kangleon and Colonel Abcede on Mindanao Island.

Her 12th, 13th and 14th runs were much the same; she went back to the Philippines, carried evacuees to safety and passed on supplies to various check posts on Mindanao Island. These were dangerous runs; once, she had to send her evacuees, mail, gathered intelligence and even her cargo to the shore, where the material was burned.

The vessel was becoming weak and she had to lighten her load then; her reserve fuel tanks were dry and she required quick repairs before she was in the clear to continue with her missions.

She also performed a role as an executioner; on her 13th patrol, she had to finish off the *USS Darter*, which had already run aground on a reef. The sub could not be recovered and the *Nautilus* was sent to drown it completely to keep it from falling into enemy hands.

Her torpedoes failed though, and even with her guns, she was not able to sink it completely, though she did it enough damage that the enemy would not recover any data from it.

The *Nautilus* performed her final patrol at Darwin, following which she was sent to Philadelphia. By this time, she had been working for decades and was quite worn down; she was decommissioned in style, celebrated with a bottle of champagne, which was broken open over her forward gun.

Finally, on the 30th of June, her name was taken off the Naval Vessel Register and she was sold to the North American Smelting Company for scrapmetal.

In her long run, the *USS Nautilus* went to war 14 times and each time, she emerged a powerful adversary to be reckoned with, even if she did not always win. She was a sub to be admired; her contribution to the War effort was integral in bringing down the Axis Powers. She set new standards in submarine warfare that few other subs could compete with!

Chapter 4: Submarines of the Royal Navy

In the previous chapter, we saw the way in which one of the American submarines – the *USS Nautilus* – took down enemy troops, fighting on the seas for almost the entire length of the Second World War.

In this chapter, we will move across to the European side of submarine warfare and take a look at Britain's Royal Navy. We will focus on one particular class of submarine – the Grampus class submarine, which were built exclusively for mine laying.

Six of these vessels were built, out of which only one survived the war. They were all named after sea creatures and were used extensive in the Mediterranean Sea, particularly to provide supplies to the island of Malta, whose conditions were tumultuous at best.

The six subs were the *HMS Porpoise, HMS Grampus, HMS Narwhal, HMS Rorqual, HMS Cachalot* and *HMS Seal*. I shall tell you the story of each of these submarines, all of which contributed to the defeat of the Axis Powers and kept the Allies going strong.

HMS Porpoise

HMS Porpoise (N14) was launched on the 30th of August in the year 1932 and fought in the war for over a decade before her untimely demise at the hands of a Japanese aircraft on the 19th of January in 1945. She was, incidentally, the last Royal Navy sub to be lost in the war.

In the year 1940, she was working in the North Sea, where she launched an attack on the German submarine *U-3*. She was not able to sink it, but dealt it severe damage. Following that battle, she took on the German minesweeper *M5* – the battle was not a direct one, though; the minesweeper was sunk by one of the many mines *HMS Porpoise* had set up.

Later, she reported that she had sighted an unknown submarine which may or may not have been the German sub *U-1*. This sub disappeared around this time. Some people speculate that it could have sunk, not from the *Porpoise's* attack, but from a mine laid out by her sister sub, the *HMS Narwhal*.

In the following years, the *Porpoise* operated on the untamed and treacherous waters of the Mediterranean Sea. In December, she took on a German passenger and cargo ship by the name of *Sebastiano Veniero*. The battle took place a few miles south of the Peloponnese peninsula and the *Porpoise's* torpedoes badly damaged the ship, which was carrying UK and Dominion prisoners of war.

Close to 300 of these prisoners were killed and the Germans had to retreat to the shore to prevent further loss of life. After this attack, the *Porpoise* went back to her usual duty of mine laying, this time off the coast of Crete.

In 1942, she took on the Italian merchant ship, *Citta di Livorno*, which she sank after a fierce battle. The Italian transport ship, *Ogaden*, also fared no better against her; but the Italian escort boat *Montanari* was beyond her capability to sink, though she did damage it.

She continued to take on more Italian ships; the merchant ship *Lerici* fell prey to her, but she was unable to sink the merchant ship *Iseo*. This particular ship damaged the *Porpoise* instead with depth charge attacks - forcing her to retreat.

As the year went on, she took on more carriers and sank them; the tanker *Giulio Giordani* fell to her as did the auxiliary patrol vessel F-39, called *Fertilia*. When she was not engaging in direct battles with these vessels, she was laying out mines to capture them;

Generale Antonio Cantore, the Italian torpedo boat, sank when it hit one of her mines. In the year 1944, she moved from the Mediterranean to the Pacific, where she took on the Japanese forces. She engaged in direct battles with a number of smaller vessels, sinking them all.

Cha 8 and *Cha 9,* which were the Japanese submarine chasers, fell to the mines laid out by the *Porpoise,* as did the army tanker *Takekun Maru.* Minesweeper *Kyo Maru No.1* and another submarine chaser, *Ch 57* were severely damaged by the *Porpoise's* mines as well.

Unfortunately for her, despite her exemplary performance in the war, she would not survive it. On the 19th of January, in the year 1945, she was laying out mines close to Panag. She completed her mission successfully and was on her way home when she was sighted by the Japanese.

They bombed her via aircraft – but she did not go down immediately! It is believed that she was damaged badly enough that she was leaking oil, but she was trying to escape the trailing Japanese forces. It took another anti-submarine craft to bring her down, though we truly do not know the exact details of her sinking.

In the end, *HMS Porpoise* took out more Axis naval vessels than anyone could expect of her. She may have just been a mine layer, but she was a force to be reckoned with.

HMS Grampus

The *HMS Grampus (N56)* was the lead ship of the entire class of mine laying submarines. She was launched on the 25th of February in the year 1936, and served off the coast of China initially, before she was moved to the Mediterranean Sea, forging her way through the war until her sinking on the 16th of June in the year 1940.

She took on big destroyers and carriers and sank them. Unlike other submarines, *HMS Grampus* truly was a creature of stealth; she rarely engaged them directly, but her mines were placed in strategic locations and took many an Axis vessel, proving her integral to the defeat of the Germans.

On the 16th of January 1940, she was under the command of Lieutenant Commander C.A. Rowe. She was laying out mines in the Augusta Area, when she was sighted by an Italian torpedo boat called *Circe*.

The boat, unfortunately, had been on an anti-submarine patrol with a couple of other similar vessels, and that meant that the *Grampus* would be engaged regardless of any consequence.

For all her strength, she was not very well prepared for a battle of this scale; for torpedo boats took her on at once, and the *Grampus* did not stand a chance. She sank very quickly and there were no survivors.

HMS Rorqual

The *HMS Rorqual (N74)* was launched on the 27th of July in the year 1936 and served through the entirety of the Second World War. She was to be the only survivor of the Grampus class submarines. She worked both in the Mediterranean Sea and in the Far East.

Initially assigned to the Mediterranean in the year 1940, the *Rorqual* was ordered to lay out mine fields under water as well as attack enemy merchant ships. A number of Italian merchant ships fell to the mines she laid out strategically, after recon – *Loasso, Celio, Leopardi,* V*erde,* to name but a few.

Italian torpedo sub that fell to her were the *Calipso,*

Generale Antonio Chinotto, Fratelli Cairoli, etc; there were Italian auxiliary minesweepers as well as German troop transport ships and French merchant vessels that sunk in the face of the mines she planted.

She dealt severe damage to a number of ships too – the Italian merchant ships, *Caffaro, Ischia and Carbonello* were among the merchant vessels that fell victim to her mines. *HMS Rorqual* also actively attacked enemy ships; she torpedoed many a boat and took out a number of them.

The Italian tanker *Laura Corrado,* the Italian submarine *Pier Capponi,* the merchant ships *Cilicia* and *Monstella* fell under her fire. She took on the German tanker *Wilhemsburg* and the French merchant ship *Nantaise,* as well as the Italian cruiser *Piero Foscari,* all of which fell to the might of her torpedoes and her other weapons. She even sank two Greek vessels from her gunfire.

In August 1940, she took on an Italian convoy, but was unable to sink them. She was unfortunately damaged herself. Having taken heavy depth charge attacks by the *Generale Achille Papa,* the Italian torpedo boat, she had to be carefully repaired before she could return to the battlefront.

In the following year, she had her biggest battle yet – she was up against the tug *Ursus*. The torpedoes would not work on the lighter boat; she was of too shallow a draught for the normal depth setting they had. In the end, the only weapon left to the *Rorqual* was her gun.

She came up to the surface of the water, around 500 yards away from her target, and open fired on the *Ursus*. She damaged the battery and the battle continued; the tug was fierce and its fire was heavy, which meant that the *Rorqual* would have to focus her fire on it, rather than the battery.

In the end, she had no choice but to dive into the water's depths, firing a torpedo on the surface. But there was a problem with it; gyro failure caused it to return to its owner and the *Rorqual* had to dive a second time to avoid getting hit by its own missile. The *Ursus*, though, did sink, and the battery was towed to Dubrovnik.

From the Mediterranean, *HMS Rorqual* moved to the Far East side of the Allied operations to take on the Japanese forces in the year 1945. She worked as part of the British Pacific Fleet, laying out minefields and gathering intelligence.

She engaged and sank three Japanese craft and coasters with her firepower and dealt severe damage to many more vessels. The war was not kind to her sisters; the *Rorqual* was the only surviving Grampus class submarine when it ended. She was sold off in the end, broken up for scrapmetal in 1946.

The HMS Rorqual was a fierce submarine, taking on the Axis Powers directly and indirectly. She did not always win, but her contribution to the war effort is undeniable.

HMS Cachalot

The HMS Cachalot (N83) was launched on the 2nd of December in the year 1937, and fought in the War in the Mediterranean as well as domestic waters, before she was sunk on the 30th of July in the year 1941.

In August 1940, she launched powerful torpedoes at the German submarine *U-51*, which sank the Nazi sub straight into the Bay of Biscay. In the following month, the minesweeper *M1604*, belonging to the auxiliary German unit sank in the face of the mines she had laid out, never having seen them coming.

HMS Cachalot continued to work in a stealthy manner,

laying out traps for unsuspecting German victims who stood no chance. It was in 1941 that she was reassigned to the Mediterranean. She left Malta on the 26th of July, headed for Alexandria.

In the afternoon, she sighted another destroyer heading towards her at breakneck pace; she had no choice but to dive to avoid it. But the destroyer was relentless; when she returned to the surface, it was there, waiting for her and launched an attack the moment she reappeared.

Cachalot tried to return to the depths of the sea, but a technical malfunction prevented her from doing so and the Italian destroyer rammed her, sinking her almost immediately. The crew escaped drowning, though as they were picked up by the Italians.

HMS Narwhal

The HMS Narwhal (N45) was launched on the 29th of August in the year 1935. She served primarily in domestic waters, and was lost at sea in July of 1940, though many speculate that she was probably sunk by a German aircraft. Her time was short, but she dealt many blows to the Axis Powers.

In February of 1940, she helped the *HMS Imogen* and *HMS Inglefield* – both war ships – in sinking the German *U-63*, close to the Shetland Islands. Following that battle, she took on the German troop transport vessel, *Buenos Aires*; she launched torpedoes at the vessel till it gave in under her fire and sank.

She also damaged the troop transport *Bahia Castillo*, which managed to reach port despite the damage done to her by the *Narwhal*, though not without significant difficulty.

The Narwhal's greatest strength, though, were her mines. She placed them strategically, after enough recon and took down a number of powerful Axis vessels with them; from German auxiliary minesweepers to submarine chasers, from armed trawlers to Swedish merchant ships – they all fell prey to the quiet mines she placed.

The Narwhal left Blyth on the 22nd of July in 1940 and three days later, vanished at sea. The report came in from an aircraft that had attacked a submarine in the rough location she was supposed to be in.

The Germans apparently believed that they were taking down the *HMS Porpoise*, but when the *Narwhal* was never heard from again, people speculate that it was she who went down instead of her sister.

HMS Seal

The HMS Seal suffered perhaps most out of all the Grampus class submarines; she was captured by the Germans and turned into a U-Boat for their forces. Launched on the 9th of December in the year 1936, she was commissioned into the Royal Navy, where she served under Lieutenant-Commander Rupert Lonsdale.

When the Second World War broke out, she was detained at Aden; her mission was to watch the Italians, since the Allied Powers were afraid that they were towing submarines despite not being part of the war yet. The *Seal* returned home after a while, and then went into service for the War, carrying out patrols and attacking German troops.

Her usual route was initially based in the Northern Sea, where she sank many a German ship. In April of 1940, when the Germans had taken over Norway, HMS *Seal* was sent to work off the Norwegian coast. She was injured severely on this mission, narrowly escaping a torpedo attack and barely making it to safety.

Later that year, she was spotted by German troops on one of her missions, and dived to avoid confrontation. Her captain, Lonsdale, realized that anti-submarine trawlers were looking for them, and diverted to the initial target area to lay down mines as per their orders.

The trawlers followed the *Seal* as she headed home and she was forced to take a long, roundabout route to try and throw them off her trail. A German patrol of anti-submarine torpedo boats were spotted and to avoid them, Lonsdale followed a zigzag course.

Unfortunately for him, they had entered an uncharted minefield and it was not long before *the Seal* was severely damaged in an explosion. Water flooded the vessel, and the crew were trapped within. Strangely though, their pursuers had not noticed their helpless state, and they set to work to try and repair the damage.

They had to wait until the sun set and it was dark to attempt rising back up to the surface. Unfortunately, their attempt was not successful; the machine was stuck and the quality of the air inside the trapped vessel was getting worse. With a few further repairs, a second attempt the rise to the surface of the sea was tried, but it failed as well.

A third attempt was also made – it also failed. It was the middle of the night and Lonsdale, a devout Christian, called his crew to him, leading them in prayer, well aware that they may not be able to survive this one.

A few thought to escape using the Davies escape gear, but many realized that it would take too long to get to safety and they would be risking flooding the entire vessel while only a few would have escaped.

One more last ditch attempt was made to rise to safety, but this failed spectacularly – the motors caught fire and the batteries were almost empty and air pressure was failing. In a wondrous miracle though, the engineer managed to make enough repairs that allowed the machine to rise to the surface.

The crew was suffering from lack of oxygen by then, and when they came to the surface, Lonsdale knew he had to risk capture and sent them to Swedish waters. German troops spotted them and attacked them; in their weakened condition, they had no choice but to surrender.

The men were wounded and dying and in an attempt to save them, Lonsdale gave up control of the submarine to the Germans, who towed the submarine to Frederikshavn, where she underwent repairs to make her sea worthy.

HMS Seal was then transformed into one of the Germans' U-Boats; she was turned against her own country and made into a weapon for the Axis Powers. However, the Germans did not succeed in their attempt to turn so faithful a vehicle – there were too many technical difficulties and the costs were too high.

She was stripped and abandoned in a dockyard, before coming to a sad end when the Allied Powers raided the dockyard and sank her. The only thing the Germans were able to get from her was the realization that the British torpedo firing device was better designed than the Germans.

Meanwhile, the crew of the *Seal,* who had been captured, was interrogated for information. Strangely though, they were not tortured unlike many of the other spies; they were held in an atmosphere of mutual respect, as prisoners of war and later, at camps.

Two members escaped and made it to the Soviet borders, but the guards – who did not understand them – robbed them, stripped them and told them to run for it. Only one of them made it home safe.

Another of the prisoners, an engineer named Don Lister, along with another engineer W.E. Hammond, also escaped, making it home safely. The rest of the officers, though, were sent to Marlag, which was a naval camp. There, they were kept as prisoners until the end of the war, though they were not tortured or hurt in any way.

In fact, it was an almost peaceful existence, until the Allies liberated them and had them return to England. Two members, though, had disappeared overboard when the machine had been taken prisoner; apart from them, the entire crew survived and came home.

Lieutenant Commander Lonsdale was the only British Captain to have surrendered his ship to the enemy – he did it for the protection of his crew, and in doing so, he ensured they did not die a bloody death at the hands of a torpedo or worse.

He was court-martialed at Portsmouth in 1946, but he was honorably acquitted, since it was his quick thinking that had saved the lives of so many innocents.

Chapter 5: HMS Perseus – The Tale of a Survivor

Launched in May of the year 1929, *HMS Perseus* hit an Italian mine, and sunk in the waters close to the Greek island of Kefalonia. Its story is one of the most controversial survival stories of the Second World War, its only survivor called a fraud initially before he was proven right.

She was a British Parthian-class submarine, built in the year 1929. She was one of the first subs to be fitted with Mark VIII torpedoes, and she put her weapons to good use. Initially, *HMS Perseus* was under the command of Peter Bartlett – she was part of the 4th Submarine Flotilla, working on the China Station.

It was not until August of 1940 that she became involved in the Second World War. Reassigned to the Mediterranean, she ferried supplies to and fro between Alexandria and Malta, which was besieged.

Her contribution to the war effort was admirable; under Lieutenant Commander Edward Christian Fredrick Nicolay, she took on a 3000 ton Italian tanker by the name of *Maya*, around 5 miles from Tendedos in September 1941 and sank her.

The very next month, she took on another merchant ship by the name of *Castellon*, west of Benghazi and sank her too, getting her commander a Distinguished Service Order.

It was in November that her end came upon her. She was instructed to patrol the waters east of Greece, in the Mediterranean and did so with a practiced ease. The waters of the Mediterranean Sea were something of a death trap from the many British submarines that patrolled them.

Underwater mines lay aplenty within the treacherous waves, and many a sub fell prey to them. Statistics tell us that two fifths of the submarines that ventured into the Mediterranean sunk; obviously, anyone on board died. Only four of those submarines ever saw soldiers escape, with the *HMS Perseus* being the most famous of all of them.

The story of her end begins when *HMS Perseus* left the British base at Malta at the end of November in the year 1941. She carried with her close to 61 people; two were passengers and the rest were crew members to keep her running.

Of the passengers, John Capes was one, a 31 year old Navy stoker, who was on his way to Alexandria. He was a student of Dulwich College and the son of a diplomat – a tall, handsome man who, as it turned out, was not even supposed to be onboard the vessel.

On the night of 6th December, *HMS Perseus* was about 2 miles off the coast of Kefalonia, recharging her batteries. Capes claimed that he was relaxing in a bunk that had been constructed from a spare torpedo tube. Without any warning, the submarine just exploded.

The picture Capes painted was a morbidly fascinating one; one moment he is relaxing in his bunk and the next, all around him, there are flames and smoke and the submarine explodes. It is almost beautiful, in a horrific way.

The vessel twisted and hit the bottom of the ocean in what Capes described as *a 'nerve-shattering jolt'*. He was thrown across the compartment even as the lights went out, leaving him in utter darkness.

What had really happened was that the submarine had hit an underwater mine – the biggest threats to submarines during the war. Covered in soot, debris and probably blood, Capes, who had realized they had hit a mine, groped for a torch and tried to save himself.

The engine room had been shut tight; the water pressure from the other side kept it closed. But he was not meant to die there. Finding a few other stokers who were showing some signs of life, he crawled towards the escape hatch.

Struggling to open it, he dragged the few survivors out with him, fitting them and himself with Davis Submarine Escape Apparatus, a rubber lung with oxygen, a mouth piece and goggles.

They were at a depth of 270 feet below sea – they were probably going to die within the murky depths, since few had ever made it out of such deep waters. Capes was freezing and terrified, but what he did not know was that the gauge was broken, showing an extra 100 feet of depth.

That didn't mean things would be easy, however; breathing became a chore even as he flooded the compartment and finally opened the escape hatch. He pushed his injured but alive companions through it, following them out.

The buoyant oxygen propelled them upward, but it was certainly not a smooth ride! The pressure made his lungs squeeze and he could not breathe. It seemed an eternity before he made it to the surface – all alone.

His companions had not survived, and he was floating by himself in the cold December sea. He had to swim to safety in the bitter cold to a band of white cliffs, where two fishermen found him lying unconscious the next morning.

The next year would be hell for Capes; he hid himself continuously to avoid the Italian occupiers. He moved from place to place, losing 70 lb, and even dyed his hair so he could pass for one of the natives. The islanders were on his side; they hid him when they could and provided him with the food he needed to survive.

Meanwhile, back at home, the Royal Navy found him gone; as the son of a diplomat, he commanded some interest. They organized a clandestine operation to find him and finally, in May of 1943, they reached him, taking him off the island on a fishing boat.

The journey back was not easy; they had to avoid enemy fleets and hence, ended up taking a long, roundabout way of 640 km into Turkey, before being able to return to the submarine service in Alexandria, where he had been initially headed.

Once he was home with his own, he was awarded a medal for his escape. But the truth of his story was doubted time and again; he was not on the crew list for the submarine, and had a history of telling stories.

Added to that was the fact that he managed to open the escape hatch from within – all submarine commanders had been ordered to bolt them shut from the outside, so that they would not lift during depth charge attacks.

He did not have any witnesses and his written accounts varied each time he told the story. He died, publicly regaled as a fraud, in 1985. It was not until 1997, when Kostas Thoctarides discovered the remains of the submarine in the waters that his story was verified.

The torpedo bun, the hatch and the compartment were exactly as Capes had described them – along with the bottle of rum he had taken a swig from before jumping to freedom through the escape hatch.

Finally, 15 years after he died, John Capes was publicly lauded as a survivor, his story accepted as the truth. He did not deal the Axis Powers any crushing blow, but he remained a shining example of the human spirit and ingenuity.

He made his way back to life, despite having nearly sunk in the sea and went back to serving in the navy, where he was awarded the British Empire Medal for his bravery and spirit.

Conclusion

Human ingenuity has ensured that over the centuries, we have progressed enough to walk on the very moon. Submarine technology, then, comes as no surprise to us. The use of subs during the wars certainly turned the tide of the battle; the Allied Powers would no doubt have lost had they not engaged in naval battles of such grandeur.

As we saw, the War was brutal and horrifying; the submarines gathered intelligence and dealt powerful blows to their enemies, who were no less the stronger. If not for their work, the world would be a very different place today, with the probability of the Axis Powers winning instead.

In the end, these subs saved many a life. Their roles in the war are downplayed – for good reason. Intelligence gathering using technology is a tricky business; it is no wonder that the Allies themselves chose to keep these stories under wraps.

What we do know is that these submarines took on the might of the most advanced technology in the world and came out victors.

If you enjoyed this book, do you think you could leave me a review on Amazon? Just search for this title and my name on Amazon to find it. Thank you so much, it is very much appreciated!

Other Books Written By Me

Below you'll find some of my other popular books that are popular on Amazon and Kindle as well. You can visit my author page on Amazon to see other work done by me. (Cyrus J. Zachary).

World War 2 Women
World War 2 Women – Book 2
World War 2 Submarines
World War 2 Submarines – Book 2
Holocaust Survivor Accounts
Holocaust Survivor Accounts – Book 2
Holocaust Rescuers
Holocaust Rescuers – Book 2

You can simply search for these titles on the Amazon website with my name to find them.

LIBRARY BUGS BOOKS

Like FREE books?

Would you like them delivered to you every week?

Do you like non-fiction books on a huge range of different topics?

We send out FREE e-books every week so we can share our books with the world!

We have FREE books every week on AMAZON that we send to our email list. If you want in, then visit the link below to sign up and sit back and wait for new books to be sent straight to your inbox!

It couldn't be simpler!

www.LibraryBugs.com

If you want FREE books delivered straight to your inbox, then visit the link above and soon you'll be receiving a great list of FREE e-books every week!

Enjoy :)

CPSIA information can be obtained
at www.ICGtesting.com
Printed in the USA
LVHW111146151020
668885LV00007B/201